THE ULTIMATE

E.
EMERIL LAGASSE

Power AirFryer 360 Plus™

COOKBOOK 2021

SPECIALS

The Most Comprehensive Guide to Mastering Your Multicooker.

Steaming, Air Frying, Grilling and Searing Your Favorite Meals in No Time!

© Copyright 2021 - Cookbook Academy by Ciro Russo

All rights reserved.

The content contained within this book may not be reproduced, duplicated or transmitted without direct written permission from the author or the publisher. Under no circumstances will any blame or legal responsibility be held against the publisher, or author, for any damages, reparation, or monetary loss due to the information contained within this book. Either directly or indirectly.

Legal Notice: This book is copyright protected. This book is only for personal use. You cannot amend, distribute, sell, use, quote or paraphrase any part, or the content within this book, without the consent of the author or publisher.

Disclaimer Notice: Please note the information contained within this document is for educational and entertainment purposes only. All effort has been executed to present accurate, up to date, and reliable, complete information. No warranties of any kind are declared or implied. Readers acknowledge that the author is not engaging in the rendering of legal, financial, medical or professional advice. The content within this book has been derived from various sources. Please consult a licensed professional before attempting any techniques outlined in this book.

By reading this document, the reader agrees that under no circumstances is the author responsible for any losses, direct or indirect, which are incurred as a result of the use of information contained within this document, including, but not limited to, — errors, omissions, or inaccuracies.

Book writing: Cookbook Academy Staff

Interior and Cover Designer: Laura Antonioli
Editor: Matt Smith
Production Manager: LP Business & Management LTD
Production Editor: Ash Rowling
Photography © 2020/2021: Janet Specter

COOKBOOK ACADEMY 2021 - by Ciro Russo

Given the great success of our publications, here are the links to other books written by us:

The Ultimate Ninja Foodi Cookbook 2021 - https://www.amazon.com/dp/B0914MSRH1
Pilot Kitchen - https://www.amazon.com/dp/B08TY8D66N

Table of Contents

Introduction • 1

Programs and Functions • 3
Benefits of Air Fryer Oven Cooking • 4
Tips for Cooking Success • 5
Guidelines for Safety and Precautions • 5
Metric Cooking Measurement vs Standard/Imperial Cooking Measurements • 9
US to Metric Cooking Conversions • 10

Fish and Seafood Dishes • 12

Broiled Scallops and Shrimp 13	*Tuna and Avocado Croquettes* 22
Garlic Roasted Seafood 14	*Cod Fillet with Curry Butter* 23
Grilled Tilapia 15	*Cod with Soy Ginger Sauce* 24
Bacon Wrapped Scallops 16	*Lemon Caper Fish Fillet* 25
Baked Lemon Butter Fish 17	*Garlic Salt and Pepper Shrimp* 26
Baked Miso Tuna 18	*Sweet and Spicy Salmon* 27
Tuna Casserole 19	*Parmesan Fish Fillet* 28
Pesto Fish Fillets with Walnuts 20	*Salmon Shioyaki* 29
Thai Fish 21	

Holiday Recipe • 30

Crispy Roasted Chickpeas 31	*Curled Zucchini Fries* 40
Crunchy Pasta Chips 32	*Cinnamon Apple Chips* 41
Breaded Avocado Fries 33	*Zucchini Pizza Boats* 42
Tomato and Cheese Pizza 34	*Roasted Shishito Peppers* 43
Mozzarella Sticks 35	*Garlic Carrot Fingers* 44
Cheesy Zucchini Chips 36	*Roasted Cauliflower* 45
Sweet Potato Fries 37	*Black Bean Burger* 46
Three-Ingredient Ravioli Bites 38	*Crispy Falafel* 47
Grilled Veggie Sandwich 39	

Lamb and Goat Dishes • 48

Roasted Lamb Chops with Garlic and Rosemary 49	*Air Fryer Feta and Lamb Frittata* 57
Lamb chops with Fennel and Orange Salad 50	*Grilled Rosemary Jerk Lamb Chops* 58
Lamb Chops in Dijon Garlic 51	*Grilled Lamb Chops with Tzatziki Sauce* 59
Braised Lamb Shanks 52	*Spiced Lamb Chops with Ginger Soy Sauce* 60
Roasted Lamb with Cumin and Lemon Crust 53	*Spicy Lamb with Lentils and Herbs* 61
Lamb Rack with Potatoes and Yogurt Mint Sauce 54	*Salt and Pepper Lamb* 62
Lamb Kebabs 55	*Barbecue Lamb Cutlets* 63
Spiced Lamb Chops with Garlic Yogurt sauce 56	

Conclusion • 64

Introduction

In recent years, air fryers have become extremely popular.

They're popular with customers because they're lightweight, flexible, and capable of handling even the most difficult recipes. Since they cook in the same way, air fryers are often compared to convection ovens.

On top of air fryers, there is normally only one heating element, while convection ovens have three.

The Emeril Lagasse Power Air Fryer 360 has five heating elements and a 1500-watt engine.

It has 12 cooking presets, a memory feature, an extra-large capacity, and a brushed stainless-steel body that is both elegant and durable.

If you're thinking of planning to get an air fryer, wait a little longer and learn why an air fryer oven might be a better option for you.

We all want to eat more nutritious foods, but we don't want to give up our favorite foods in the process!

The Emeril Lagasse Power Airfryer 360 does just that: allows you to cook, bake, roast, and more delicious meals right on your kitchen countertop—without the use of oils, fats, or grease.

This powerful countertop oven, which uses a 360° whirlpool of superheated air to cook your food, can replace up to nine different kitchen cooking accessories, such as a convection oven, toaster oven, and other appliances, thus lowering the number of calories by almost every meal!

How Does the Emeril Lagasse Power Air Fryer 360 Work?

The hot air created by the heating elements is used to cook the food in air fryers. Convection fans circulate hot air to cook the food uniformly on all sides, similarly to convection ovens.

For best results, the 5 heating elements of the Emeril Lagasse Power Air Fryer 360 will be activated by the device depending on the cooking function chosen.

Air fried, toast, pizza, broil, bake, bagel, rotisserie, dehydrate, roast, reheat, warm, and slow cook are among the 12 presets. Between the top and bottom heating elements, there are four levels where you can position your tray, rack, or pan while cooking. For easy reference, the guide is also printed on the glass door.

Broiling and dehydrating are best done in the first position, closest to the top heating element. Toast, bagel, broil, air fry, dehydrate, and rotisserie functions are all available in the second position. The reheat, bake, roast, steam, pizza, and dehydrate functions are all found in the third position. Finally, the slow cook feature is found in the fourth position.

Programs and Functions

Air fry
The air fry feature will use the side heating elements for operation, with the air fry fans switched on. In the second location, position the crisper tray. It's better to use the baking tray and pizza rack just below the crisper tray while cooking foods with enough moisture or fat content that may drip during the cooking process.

Toast
To make those toasted brown colorations on both sides, the toast feature uses the top and bottom heating elements. From one to five, you can choose how dark your toast should be. It can toast six slices of loaf bread at once.

Bagel
The top and bottom heating elements are used in the bagel feature, while the air frying fans are switched off. You can fit up to six slices of bagels and choose the toast's darkness, just like with the toast feature. When this function is used, the pizza rack is moved to the second position.

Pizza
The top and bottom heating elements are used for the pizza function. The bottom heating unit crisps the dough, while the top heats the toppings and melts the cheese. During the cooking process, the air frying fans can be turned on.

Bake
The bake feature uses the top and bottom heating elements and allows you to switch on or off the air frying fans, it is ideal for baking pastries, cakes, and pies.

Broil
Broiling and melting cheeses over burgers, sandwiches, or fries is easy with the broil function. While the air frying fan is turned off, it uses the top heating element. To get the best results, the pizza rack should be positioned near the top heating part.

Rotisserie
The top and bottom heating components, as well as the revolving spit accessory, are used in the rotisserie function. Food turns brown and crispy on the outside while remaining sweet and juicy on the inside.

Slow cook
The top and bottom heating elements are used in the slow cook function. It works well with a Dutch oven, the baking dish with lid, or any other similar cooking pot for making

tender pulled pork or beef brisket. The Power Air Fryer 360 can cook for up to 10 hours on "slow cooking" mode.

Roast
The roast feature is the better preset for cooking large cuts of meat since it equally cooks the meat on all sides. It also makes use of the heating elements on the top and bottom.

Dehydrate
Fruits, vegetables, and meat can all be dried using the dehydrate feature. To uniformly dry out the ingredients, it only uses the top heating element with the air frying fans switched on during the process.

Reheat
With the option to switch on the air frying fans, the reheat mechanism uses both the top and bottom heating components. It's perfect for reheating food that doesn't need to be seared.

Warm
With the air frying fans turned off, the warm mechanism uses the top and bottom heating elements. It's perfect for keeping food at a comfortable temperature until you're ready to serve it.

Benefits of Air Fryer Oven Cooking

Compact and versatile
Air fryer ovens, unlike traditional ovens, can comfortably fit on your kitchen countertop and be stored when not in use. They're adaptable and can do a variety of tasks in the kitchen.

Energy-efficient
Air fryer ovens heat up and cook 40% faster than bulky, regular ovens.

Rotisserie function
It allows you to easily cook a whole chicken, a leg of lamb, a big chunk of beef, or multiple kebabs. Some air fryer ovens have a rotisserie spit or drum, which makes roasting meat or other foods a breeze.

Bigger capacity than standard air fryers
The interior has several layers, allowing you to cook several foods at the same time. A whole chicken can be cooked in under an hour using just the Power Air Fryer 360.

Requires much less oil than traditional cookers
Air fryers use 70% less oil than regular deep fryers, making them a more cost-effective and healthier option.

Easy to clean

Stainless steel or aluminum are used in the majority of air fryer toast ovens. They are not only fashionable and beautiful, but they are also long-lasting and food-safe. The cooking chamber and removable parts are normally made of stainless steel or coated with a non-stick coating. The oven racks, air fry baskets, and other accessories are also dishwasher-safe.

Tips for Cooking Success

- Before using the appliance, make sure you complete the necessary initial steps.

- Foods with a smaller size will take less time to prepare. Cutting food into equal sizes will ensure easier and more even cooking, which will help you save time in the kitchen.

- A crispier texture can be achieved by spraying, misting, or gently brushing food with oil before cooking. Ensure that you don't add too much or it will get soggy.

- To achieve even cooking, turn or stir the food halfway through the cooking time.

- You can use the air fryer oven to make snack or pastry recipes that would normally be made in a conventional oven.

- Make sure the food isn't overcrowded. Allow some space between pans, particularly when cooking food with a coating or batter, to allow hot air to circulate and evenly cook the food.

- When making recipes that call for high temperatures, use oils with a high smoking point or that can withstand high temperatures. Avocado, peanut, and grapeseed oils are all good examples. The smoke point of olive oil is low. If you must use olive oil, use extra light olive oil, which has a higher smoke point and won't dry out the food until it finishes cooking.

- Do not put cooking trays or pans directly on the bottom heating elements, as this will prevent hot air from circulating properly and cooking the food.

- Oil and grease crumbs and drippings can cause smoke and burn. Place a baking tray lined with foil and parchment paper underneath the crisper tray or baking pan to avoid this.

Guidelines for Safety and Precautions

Reading the user manual is one of the first things you should do after getting your device. Not only will it advise you on the proper use, but it will also protect you from any accidents while using it.

For those of you who may have misplaced the instructions in the package (or for those who are simply a little distracted...) here are some of the guidelines to remember when using the Emeril Lagasse power air fryer.

DO

- This appliance is only meant to be used indoors.
- Only people with normal auditory, emotional, and physical abilities who have read and understood the manual should use the appliance.
- Keep out of wet areas and hot surfaces like stovetops.
- Place the air fryer oven on a counter or table that is stable, level, and heat-resistant.
- Leave at least five inches of clearance around the oven during service, as it can heat up and release steam.
- Once the oven is in operation, make sure there is no food protruding from it.
- When removing food from the oven, use oven mitts, gloves, or dish towels.
- Make sure the appliance is completely turned off before carefully unplugging it.
- After each use, unplug and clean the appliance.
- When the drip tray is halfway full, remove it and clean it.
- When removing any hot oil from the unit, use caution.
- Allow at least 30 minutes for the machine to cool fully after unplugging it.

DO NOT

- Use an extension cord with this appliance to prevent accidents.
- Use the unit without the drip tray installed.
- Place anything on top of the oven.
- Block the air vents, especially while the unit is turned on.
- Put flammable materials near or on top of the air fryer oven such as paper, plastic, curtains, towels, etc.
- Connect to an electrical outlet that is already used by other appliances as it may cause it to overload.
- Connect with an electrical outlet other than a 2-prong grounded 120V.
- Modify the plug or any part of the unit.
- Use accessories that are not recommended by the manufacturer.
- Clean parts with metal scouring pads and abrasive chemicals.
- Submerge the unit in water.
- Line the drip tray with foil.

- Use metal utensils or cutleries to prevent electric shock.

Follow the steps below when you are about to use the unit for the first time.

1. All packaging materials, labels, and stickers must be removed and properly disposed of before using your air fryer oven for the first time.
2. Use warm water and a mild detergent to clean the crisper tray, drip tray, pizza rack, baking pan, rotisserie spit, and rotisserie stand. Thoroughly dry the region.
3. With the aid of a moist cloth and a mild detergent, clean the exterior and interior. Make sure the fabric isn't too damp, as this could cause water to soak into some electrical components.
4. Connect the device to an outlet on the kitchen counter.
5. Burn off any protective coating or oil by preheating the oven for a few minutes. During this stage, it's common for some smoke to appear.
6. Turn the device off, unplug it, and allow it to cool fully. With a damp rag, wipe the interior and exterior once more.

Measurement Conversion

Often you'll come across a fantastic recipe that uses unfamiliar measurements, such as mL instead of cups. Conversion charts, whether metric, imperial, or gas label, come in handy in this case, assisting you in creating whatever recipe you want to try.

When cooking, it's a good idea to have a kitchen scale and a set of full measuring cups on hand to ensure that the ingredients are correctly measured.

Abbreviations for Cooking Measurements

When you're following a recipe, it's critical to know what the cooking abbreviations mean. When writing out recipes, many authors use shorthand, and if you don't know what it means, you may make a few mistakes.

Abbreviations for Imperial/Standard Measurement

lb = Pound
qt = Quart
tsp = Teaspoon
pt = Pint
Oz = Ounce
c = Cup
fl. Oz = Fluid ounce
gal = Gallon
Tbsp = Tablespoon (also TB, Tbl)

Abbreviations for Metric Measurement

kg = kilogram
g = grams
l = liter
mL = Milliliter

Liquid Ingredients vs. Dry Ingredients Measurement

When it comes to weighing, dry and liquid ingredients should be handled differently. Measuring cups and spoon sets are commonly used to measure dry ingredients, while liquid measuring cups are used to measure liquids. Exact measurements can be achieved by using the appropriate measuring instruments.

To get the most precise number when measuring dry ingredients, fill the cup to the brim and scrape the excess off the end. A liquid measuring cup cannot be used for this, which is why it should not be used. Although a liquid measuring cup will give you a more precise liquid measurement, when a recipe calls for small quantities of liquid, you will need to use measuring spoons instead.

These recommendations are particularly useful when preparing recipes that necessitate precise measurements.

Fluid Ounces vs Ounces

The difference between using ounces and fluid ounces comes down to the difference between liquid and dry ingredients. Weight is measured in ounces, while volume is measured in fluid ounces. Liquid ingredients are measured in fluid ounces, while dry ingredients are measured in ounces (by weight) (by volume). So just because a recipe calls for 8 ounces of flour doesn't mean you'll need 1 cup.

Most American recipes (using the standard/imperial system) would list dry ingredients in cups/tablespoons/etc. instead of ounces. Remember this when you're weighing your ingredients!

Basic Kitchen Conversions & Equivalents

In the kitchen, having a basic understanding of cooking measurements and conversions is important. When you're following a recipe, it's important to understand what everything means. You can't always find the darn tablespoon to measure out your ingredients, so you have to wing it... However, if you know that 1 tablespoon equals 3 teaspoons, you can weigh with confidence!

Simply follow these kitchen conversion charts, and you'll have them memorized in no time, just like your school's multiplication tables.

Conversion Chart for Dry Measurements.

3 teaspoons is equivalent to 1 tablespoon = 1/16 cup

6 teaspoons is equivalent to 2 tablespoons = ⅛ cup

12 teaspoons is equivalent to 4 tablespoons = ¼ cup

24 teaspoons is equivalent to 8 tablespoons = ½ cup

36 teaspoons is equivalent to 12 tablespoons = ¾ cup

48 teaspoons is equivalent to 16 tablespoons = 1 cup

Measurements Conversion Chart for Liquid

8 fluid ounces = 1 cup = ½ pint = ¼ quart

16 fluid ounces = 2 cups = 1 pint = ½ quart

32 fluid ounces = 4 cups = 2 pints = 1 quart = ¼ gallon

128 fluid ounces = 16 cups = 8 pints = 4 quarts = 1 gallon

Butter

1 cup butter = 2 sticks = 230 grams = 8 ounces = 8 tablespoons

Metric Cooking Measurement vs Standard Imperial Cooking Measurements

Metric to US Cooking Conversions

Oven Temperatures
- 120 c = 250 F
- 160 c = 320 F
- 180 c = 350 F
- 205 c = 400 F
- 220 c = 425 F

Baking in grams
- 1 cup heavy cream = 235 grams
- 1 cup sugar = 150 grams
- 1 cup powdered sugar = 160 grams
- 1 cup Flour = 140 grams

Volume

- 1 milliliter is equivalent to 1/5 teaspoon
- 5 ml is equivalent to 1 teaspoon
- 15 ml is equivalent to 1 tablespoon
- 240 ml is equivalent to 1 cup or 8 fluid ounces
- 1 liter is equivalent to 34 fl. ounces

Weight

- 1 gram = .035 ounces
- 100 grams = 3.5 ounces
- 500 grams = 1.1 pounds
- 1 kilogram = 35 ounces

US to Metric Cooking Conversions

- 1 pound = 454 grams
- 1 gallon (16 cups) = 3.8 liters
- 1 cup = 237 ml
- 1 tsp = 5 ml
- 1 tbsp = 15 ml
- 1 fl ounce = 30 ml
- 1 pint (2 cups) = 473 ml
- 1 quart (4 cups) = .95 liter
- 1 oz = 28 grams
- 1/5 tsp = 1 ml

What is 1 Cup Equivalent to?

Knowing what 1 cup equals is useful because, even if you don't have any kitchen measuring instruments, most people would have a 1 cup measurement. It can also be useful for cooking conversions while halving or doubling recipes. Just keep in mind that 1 cup equals these different measurements, so everything in this chart is equivalent!

- 1 cup = 8 fluid ounces
- 1 cup = 16 tablespoons
- 1 cup = 48 teaspoons
- 1 cup = ½ pint
- 1 cup = ¼ quart
- 1 cup = 1/16 gallon
- 1 cup = 240 ml

Baking Pan Conversions

(The cups denote the amount of batter that will fit into the pan.)

- 9-inch square pan = 8 cups
- 10-inch bundt pan = 12 cups
- 9 x 5 inch loaf pan = 8 cups
- 9-inch round cake pan = 12 cups
- 10-inch tube pan = 16 cups
- 9-inch springform pan = 10 cups

Conversion of Common Baking Measurements to Ounces

- 1 cup unsifted powdered sugar = 4.4oz
- 1 cup all-purpose flour = 4.5oz
- 1 cup rolled oats = 3oz
- 1 large egg = 1.7oz
- 1 cup milk = 8oz

- 1 cup heavy cream = 8.4oz
- 1 cup granulated sugar = 7.1oz
- 1 cup packed brown sugar = 7.75oz
- 1 cup vegetable oil = 7.7oz
- 1 cup butter = 8oz

Ratings

In all of our cookbooks you'll find a grade of evaluation on each individual recipe called "Ratings".

The "Ratings" goes from 1 to 5 stars and it is determined by the complexity of the dish and the time you'll need to prepare it.

1 star will indicate a very quick and easy meal, while 5 stars will be a more complex recipe with higher preparation time needed.

We wanted to offer you this method of evaluating on every dish in order to make it even easier for you to choose the most suitable recipes according to your time availability.

Cookbook Academy Team

Fish and Seafood Dishes

Broiled Scallops and Shrimp

Preparation time MINUTES | **Cooking time** MINUTES | **Servings** 6

Ratings
★★★
★

Ingredients

1/4 cup butter, melted
1 tablespoon lemon juice
1 tablespoon Worcestershire sauce
1/3 cup dry white wine
3 cloves garlic, crushed
Pinch red pepper flakes
Salt and pepper to taste
1 lb. shrimp, peeled and deveined
1 lb. scallops
1 cup cherry tomatoes, sliced in half
5 oz. baby spinach

Directions

1. Combine butter, lemon juice, Worcestershire sauce, wine, garlic, red pepper, salt and pepper in a bowl.
2. Toss shrimp and scallops in the bowl.
3. Transfer to the air fryer oven.
4. Choose broil setting.
5. Broil for 3 minutes.
6. Stir in tomatoes and spinach.
7. Broil for another 2 minutes.

Serving suggestion

Serve with slices of French bread.

Tip

You can also use other leafy greens in place of spinach.

Garlic Roasted Seafood

Preparation time 25 MINUTES | **Cooking time** 15 MINUTES | **Servings** 4

Ratings
★★★

Ingredients

1/2 cup butter
3 cloves garlic, crushed
1 tablespoon lemon juice
2 teaspoons lemon zest
1 teaspoon smoked paprika
1 cup shrimp, peeled and deveined
2 squids, cleaned
12 mussels
2 cups baby potatoes
2 cobs corn, sliced

Directions

1. Combine butter, garlic, lemon juice, lemon zest and paprika in a bowl.
2. Arrange the seafood in a baking pan.
3. Drizzle with the butter sauce.
4. Place inside the air fryer oven.
5. Select roast option.
6. For 15 minutes cook at 400 degrees F, stirring once or twice.

Serving suggestion

Sprinkle with chopped parsley.

Tip

Throw away mussels that did not open during cooking.

Grilled Tilapia

Preparation time
35 MINUTES

Cooking time
15 MINUTES

Servings
2

Ratings
★★★

Ingredients

1 tilapia

Marinade

2 tablespoons oil
5 cloves garlic
1 onion, sliced
1/2 teaspoon curry powder
2 seasoning cubes
2 sprigs fresh thyme
1 teaspoon nutmeg
Salt and pepper to taste

Directions

1. Add marinade ingredients to a blender.
2. Process until smooth.
3. Make several slits on both sides of fish.
4. Coat with the marinade.
5. Cover and refrigerate for 30 minutes.
6. Place the fish inside the air fryer oven.
7. Select grill setting.
8. Cook at 350 degrees F for 15 minutes per side.

Serving suggestion

Serve on top of leafy greens and sliced tomatoes.

Tip

You can also add chili powder to the marinade.

Bacon Wrapped Scallops

Preparation time
15 MINUTES

Cooking time
5 MINUTES

Servings
4

Ratings

★ ★ ★
★

Ingredients

16 scallops
8 slices bacon, sliced into 2
1/4 teaspoon paprika
Pinch pepper

Directions

1. Wrap the scallops with bacon slices.
2. Secure with toothpicks.
3. Season with pepper and paprika.
4. Preheat your air fryer oven to 350 degrees F.
5. Choose air fry setting.
6. Cook for 3 minutes.
7. Flip and cook for another 3 minutes.

Serving suggestion

Serve immediately.

Tip

You can also pre-cook bacon by air frying at 400 degrees F for 3 minutes before wrapping it around the scallop.

Baked Lemon Butter Fish

Preparation time
5 MINUTES

Cooking time
12 MINUTES

Servings
4

Ratings
★ ★ ★ ★

Ingredients

4 white fish fillets
1/4 cup butter, melted
3 cloves garlic, minced
2 tablespoons lemon juice
1 teaspoon lemon zest
Salt and pepper to taste
Lemon slices

Directions

1. Choose bake option in your air fryer oven.
2. Preheat it to 425 degrees F.
3. Arrange the fish fillets in a baking pan.
4. Combine the remaining ingredients except lemon slices in a bowl.
5. Pour the mixture over the fish.
6. Top with the lemon slices.
7. Bake in the air fryer oven for 6 minutes per side.

Serving suggestion

Garnish with chopped parsley.

Tip

You can also use garlic powder instead of minced garlic.

Baked Miso Tuna

Preparation time
1 HOUR

Cooking time
15 MINUTES

Servings
4

Ratings
★ ★

Ingredients

2 tuna steaks
1/2 tablespoon miso paste
2 tablespoons mirin
1 tablespoon garlic, minced
1 teaspoon rice wine
1/2 teaspoon vinegar

Directions

1. Add tuna steaks to a baking pan.
2. Combine remaining ingredients in a bowl.
3. Pour the marinade over the tuna.
4. Cover and refrigerate for 1 hour.
5. Transfer to the air fryer oven.
6. Choose bake setting.
7. Cook at 360 degrees F for 5 to 7 minutes per side.

Serving suggestion

Garnish with chopped green onion.

Tip

Tuna steaks should be at least ½ inch thick.

Tuna Casserole

Preparation time: 5 MINUTES

Cooking time: 10 MINUTES

Servings: 2

Ratings: ★★★★

Ingredients

Casserole

- 10 oz. canned tuna flakes, drained
- 1/4 cup Mexican cheese blend, shredded
- 1/4 cup onion, chopped
- 1/4 teaspoon onion powder
- 1/4 cup celery, chopped
- 2 tablespoons mayonnaise
- 1/4 cup breadcrumbs
- 1 tablespoon Parmesan cheese
- Salt and pepper to taste

Topping

- 1/4 cup cheddar cheese, grated

Directions

1. Combine all the casserole ingredients in a baking pan.
2. Top with the grated cheese.
3. Set your air fryer oven to bake.
4. Preheat your air fryer oven to 380 degrees F for 5 minutes.
5. Position the baking pan inside the air fryer oven.
6. Bake for 6 to 10 minutes or until cheese has melted.

Serving suggestion

Sprinkle with chopped green onion.

Tip

You can also add a little cayenne pepper to the casserole if you like.

Pesto Fish Fillets with Walnuts

Preparation time: 20 MINUTES

Cooking time: 10 MINUTES

Servings: 2

Ratings

★

Ingredients

2 salmon fillets
Salt and pepper to taste
2 tablespoons pesto sauce
1 tablespoon mayonnaise
1/4 cup walnuts, chopped

Directions

1. Season fish with salt and pepper.
2. Mix pesto and mayo.
3. Spread pesto sauce on top of fish.
4. Top with walnuts.
5. Place in the air crisper tray.
6. Choose air fry setting.
7. Place the fish in the air fryer oven.
8. Cook at 380 degrees F for 10 minutes.

Serving suggestion

Sprinkle with Parmesan cheese before serving.

Tip

Dry the fish thoroughly with paper towel before seasoning.

Thai Fish

Preparation time 5 MINUTES | **Cooking time** 10 MINUTES | **Servings**

Ratings
★★★
★★

Ingredients

1 teaspoon soy sauce
2 teaspoons fish sauce
1 tablespoon oyster sauce
1 clove garlic, minced
1/2 tablespoon lime juice
1 tablespoon brown sugar
2 flounder fillets

Directions

1. Combine soy sauce, fish sauce, oyster sauce, garlic, lime juice and brown sugar in a bowl.
2. Brush both sides of fish with this mixture.
3. Add the fish fillets to the air fryer oven.
4. Set the air fryer oven to roast.
5. Cook at 370 degrees F for 5 minutes per side.

Serving suggestion

Sprinkle with thinly sliced fresh basil leaves.

Tip

Use low-sodium fish sauce and soy sauce.

Tuna and Avocado Croquettes

Preparation time
5 MINUTES

Cooking time
10 MINUTES

Servings
4

Ratings
★ ★ ★
★

Ingredients

2 cups canned tuna flakes
1/4 teaspoon onion powder
1/2 avocado, pitted
2 tablespoons lemon juice
1/4 cup roasted almonds, chopped
1/2 cup breadcrumbs
Salt and pepper to taste

Directions

1. Combine all the ingredients in a bowl.
2. Form balls from the mixture.
3. Set your air fryer oven to air fry.
4. Place the tuna balls in the air crisper tray.
5. Cook at 380 degrees F for 8 minutes or until golden.

Serving suggestion

Serve with marinara dip.

Tip

You can also add chopped onion in the mixture.

Cod Fillet with Curry Butter

Preparation time
10 MINUTES

Cooking time
10 MINUTES

Servings
2

Ratings
★★★
★

Ingredients

1 tablespoon butter, melted
1/4 teaspoon curry powder
1/8 teaspoon paprika
Pinch garlic powder
Salt to taste
2 cod fillets

Directions

1. Combine butter, curry powder, paprika, garlic powder and salt in a bowl.
2. Coat cod fillets with this mixture.
3. Add cod fillets to the air fryer oven.
4. Set it to roast.
5. Cook at 360 degrees F for 4 to 5 minutes per side.
6. Drizzle with cooking liquid and serve.

Serving suggestion

Sprinkle with thinly sliced basil.

Tip

Add more curry powder if you like your fish spicier.

Cod with Soy Ginger Sauce

Preparation time
5 MINUTES

Cooking time
10 MINUTES

Servings
2

Ratings
★★★
★

Ingredients

1 tablespoon butter, melted
1-1/2 tablespoons rice wine
2 teaspoons honey
1 tablespoon soy sauce
2 cod fillets
1 tablespoon ginger, sliced thinly

Directions

1. Combine butter, rice wine, honey and soy sauce in a bowl.
2. Place the cod fillets on top of a foil sheet.
3. Sprinkle the ginger slices on top.
4. Pour the butter sauce over the fish.
5. Fold the foil to wrap the fish.
6. Pinch sides to seal.
7. Place in the air fryer oven.
8. Select air fry setting.
9. Cook at 360 degrees F for 10 minutes.

Serving suggestion

Garnish with cilantro.

Tip

You can also add sliced onions inside the packet.

Lemon Caper Fish Fillet

Preparation time
5 MINUTES

Cooking time
6 MINUTES

Servings
2

Ratings
★ ★ ★
★

Ingredients

2 cod fillets
Salt and pepper to taste
1-1/2 tablespoons butter
1/2 teaspoon lemon zest
3 tablespoons lemon juice
1 tablespoon capers

Directions

1. Spray fish with oil.
2. Season with salt and pepper.
3. Place the fish inside the air fryer oven.
4. Choose air fry setting.
5. Cook at 360 degrees F for 3 minutes per side.
6. In a pan over medium heat, add the butter.
7. Once melted, stir in lemon zest, lemon juice and capers.
8. Simmer for 1 minute.
9. Transfer fish to a serving plate.
10. Pour sauce over the fish and serve.

Serving suggestion

Sprinkle with pepper.

Tip

Extend cooking time until fish is flaky.

Garlic Salt and Pepper Shrimp

Preparation time
5 MINUTES

Cooking time
6 MINUTES

Servings
8

Ratings
★★★
★

Ingredients

16 shrimp
2 teaspoons olive oil
1 teaspoon rice wine
Salt and pepper to taste
2 cloves garlic, minced

Directions

1. Combine all the ingredients in a bowl.
2. Set the air fryer oven to air fry.
3. Add the shrimp mixture to the air crisper tray.
4. Cook at 400 degrees F for 3 minutes per side.
5. Mix all ingredients together and let sit for 5 minutes.

Serving suggestion

Garnish with crispy garlic bits.

Tip

You can also use frozen shrimp for this recipe.

Sweet and Spicy Salmon

Preparation time
5 MINUTES

Cooking time
15 MINUTES

Servings
4

Ratings
★ ★ ★
★

Ingredients

4 salmon fillets
1 tablespoon butter, melted
1/2 tablespoon chili powder
1/4 teaspoon paprika
2 tablespoons brown sugar
1 teaspoon cumin
Pinch cayenne pepper
Salt and pepper to taste

Directions

1. Brush both sides of salmon with butter.
2. Mix the remaining ingredients in a bowl.
3. Sprinkle salmon with the spice mixture.
4. Add salmon to the air fryer oven.
5. Choose roast setting.
6. Preheat your air fryer oven to 380 degrees F for 5 minutes.
7. For 6 minutes per side cook the salmon.

Serving suggestion

Let rest for 5 minutes before serving.

Tip

You can also brush with melted butter in between cooking.

Parmesan Fish Fillet

Preparation time: 10 MINUTES

Cooking time: 10 MINUTES

Servings: 2

Ratings: ★★★★

Ingredients

1/4 teaspoon paprika
1/2 teaspoon Italian seasoning
Salt and pepper to taste
2 fish fillets
1/4 cup Parmesan cheese, grated

Directions

1. Mix paprika, Italian herbs, salt and pepper in a bowl.
2. Season fish with the mixture.
3. Cover with Parmesan cheese.
4. Set the air fryer oven to bake.
5. Preheat it to 370 degrees F for 5 minutes.
6. Place the fish inside the air fryer oven.
7. Cook for 5 minutes per side.

Serving suggestion

Garnish with chopped green onion.

Tip

You can also add breadcrumbs to the breading.

Salmon Shioyaki

Preparation time
6 HOURS

Cooking time
10 MINUTES

Servings
4

Ratings
★

Ingredients

4 salmon fillets
2 tablespoons rice wine
4 teaspoons salt

Directions

1. Coat salmon with rice wine.
2. Let sit for 10 minutes.
3. Sprinkle with salt.
4. Place inside a sealable plastic bag.
5. Refrigerate for 6 hours.
6. Transfer salmon to the air crisper tray.
7. Choose air fry setting.
8. Cook the salmon at 400 degrees F for 4 to 5 minutes per side.

Serving suggestion

Garnish with lime wedges.

Tip

Dry salmon with paper towel before seasoning.

Holiday Recipe

Crispy Roasted Chickpeas

Preparation time
5 MINUTES

Cooking time
10 MINUTES

Servings
3

Ratings
★

Ingredients

425 grams chickpeas, drained and patted dry

1 tablespoon olive oil

Salt to taste

Directions

1. Lightly grease the chickpeas with olive oil.
2. Add salt to taste.
3. In one layer spread the chickpeas on a sheeted baking pan.
4. Select the roast function in your air fryer oven.
5. Cook for 10 minutes at 390°F.

Serving suggestion

Put in a take-away container and snack away throughout the day. Also try them as toppings on your salad or soup.

Tip

Store in a paper bag or loosely covered container at room temperature for up to a week.

Crunchy Pasta Chips

Preparation time
30 MINUTES

Cooking time
10 MINUTES

Servings
2

Ratings
★★★
★

Ingredients

1 tablespoon nutritional yeast
1-1/2 teaspoon Italian seasoning
Salt to taste
1 tablespoon olive oil
2 cups dry whole wheat bowtie pasta, cooked and drained

Directions

1. Combine the nutritional yeast, Italian seasoning, salt, and olive oil in a bowl.
2. Toss the pasta with the mixture.
3. Cook at 390°F for 10 minutes.
4. Shake the air fryer to cook evenly.

Serving suggestion

Enjoy as is or with your favorite dip.

Tip

Let the chips cool down completely to enjoy their maximum crunchiness.

Breaded Avocado Fries

Preparation time: 10 MINUTES

Cooking time: 10 MINUTES

Servings: 4

Ratings: ★★★★

Ingredients

1 cup aquafaba
1/2 cup panko breadcrumbs
Salt to taste
1 Haas avocado, peeled and sliced

Directions

1. Put aquafaba into a shallow bowl.
2. In a separate container, mix the panko breadcrumbs and salt.
3. Dip the avocado slices in aquafaba, and then dredge them with the panko and salt mixture.
4. Arrange the slices in a single layer on a greased baking sheet.
5. Select the bake function on your air fryer oven.
6. Bake for 10 minutes at 390°F.

Serving suggestion

Serve immediately with a creamy sauce such as spicy mayo or ranch dressing.

Tip

For best results, use a slightly under-ripe avocado—neither too firm nor too soft.

Tomato and Cheese Pizza

Preparation time
5 MINUTES

Cooking time
10 MINUTES

Servings
2

Ratings
★★★
★★

Ingredients

12 inches pizza dough
1 teaspoon olive oil
1 tablespoon tomato sauce
Buffalo mozzarella

Directions

1. Spread the dough out to the size of two personal pan pizzas.
2. Lightly brush the dough with olive oil.
3. Spread a layer of tomato sauce.
4. Top with chunks of buffalo mozzarella.
5. Place the dough on a greased baking pan.
6. Select the bake function on your air fryer oven.
7. Bake at 375°F for 7 minutes.

Serving suggestion

Top with grated Parmesan cheese, basil, and pepper flakes.

Tip

The pizza will be piping hot so allow ample time for it to cool down before taking a bite.

Mozzarella Sticks

Preparation time
2 HOURS 15 MINUTES

Cooking time
10 MINUTES

Servings
2

Ratings
★

Ingredients

6 mozzarella sticks
3 tablespoons all-purpose flour
2 eggs, beaten
1 cup panko breadcrumbs

Directions

1. Freeze mozzarella sticks for at least 2 hours.
2. Set the flour, eggs, and panko in separate bowls.
3. Coat the mozzarella sticks in flour, and then dip them in egg, and then panko.
4. Dip the sticks in egg, and then panko again.
5. Arrange the sticks in a single layer on a baking sheet.
6. Select the bake function on your air fryer oven.
7. Bake at 400°F for 6 minutes.

Serving suggestion

Serve with warm marinara sauce.

Tip

Keep an eye while cooking, and do not let the cheese ooze out.

Cheesy Zucchini Chips

Preparation time
10 MINUTES

Cooking time
15 MINUTES

Servings
4

Ratings
★★★
★

Ingredients

1 medium zucchini, thinly sliced
1 large egg, beaten
1 cup panko breadcrumbs
3/4 Parmesan cheese, grated
Cooking spray

Directions

1. Combine the panko and cheese.
2. In the beaten eggdip the zucchini slices, and then coat with the mixture.
3. Lightly grease with cooking spray.
4. Cook using the bake function on your air fryer oven at 350°F for 12 minutes.

Serving suggestion

You can use ranch dressing or marinara sauce for dipping.

Tip

Flip with tongs to cook evenly.

Sweet Potato Fries

Preparation time
5 MINUTES

Cooking time
20 MINUTES

Servings
4

Ratings
★ ★ ★
★

Ingredients

1/4 teaspoon paprika
1/2 teaspoon garlic powder
1/2 teaspoon fine sea salt
2 medium sweet potatoes, cut into strips
1 tablespoon olive oil

Directions

1. Add all the ingredients except for the sweet potatoes and oil.
2. Coat the fries with oil and the mixture.
3. Set the air fryer oven to bake function at 380°F.
4. Cook for 18 minutes.

Serving suggestion

Garnish with parsley and serve with ketchup for dipping.

Tip

Keep an eye will cooking as the fries will brown at different rates depending on the size.

Three Ingredient Ravioli Bites

Preparation time
5 MINUTES

Cooking time
5 MINUTES

Servings
2

Ratings
★★★
★★

Ingredients

12 frozen ravioli
1/2 cup buttermilk
1/2 cup Italian breadcrumbs

Directions

1. Dip ravioli into the buttermilk.
2. Coat with breadcrumbs.
3. Cook using bake function at 400°F for 6 minutes or until golden brown.

Serving suggestion

Serve immediately with marinara sauce.

Tip

They can also be kept inside the fridge for up to 3 months.

Grilled Veggie Sandwich

Preparation time
35 MINUTES

Cooking time
10 MINUTES

Servings
4

Ratings
★★★

Ingredients

1 tablespoon lemon juice
3 cloves garlic, minced
1/4 cup mayonnaise
1 small yellow squash, sliced
red onion, sliced
bell pepper, sliced
1 small zucchini, sliced
12 focaccia bread, sliced
1/2 cup crumbled feta cheese

Directions

1. Mix the lemon juice, garlic and mayonnaise; and then set aside in refrigerator.
2. Brush all the vegetables with olive oil.
3. Cook using grill function at high setting for 6 minutes, and then set aside.
4. Spread mayonnaise mix and cheese on the bread.
5. Grill for 2 to 3 minutes.
6. Transfer to plate and layer with the grilled veggies.

Serving suggestion

Top with alfalfa sprouts.

Tip

You may also enjoy it as an open sandwich.

Curled Zucchini Fries

Preparation time
20 MINUTES

Cooking time
10 MINUTES

Servings
4

Ratings
★ ★ ★
★

Ingredients

1 cup panko breadcrumbs

1/2 cup Parmesan cheese, grated

1 teaspoon Italian seasoning

1 large zucchini, sliced using spiralizer

1 large egg, beaten

Directions

1. Mix the panko, cheese and Italian seasoning in a large resealable plastic bag.
2. Dip the zucchini in the beaten egg, and then put inside the bag with the mix to coat.
3. Use the bake function at 400°F for 10 minutes.

Serving suggestion

Serve with a zesty ranch dipping sauce.

Tip

Cook in batches for evenly crisped results.

Cinnamon Apple Chips

Preparation time
5 MINUTES

Cooking time
15 MINUTES

Servings
2

Ratings
★★★

Ingredients

2 medium apples, thinly sliced

Directions

1. Sprinkle the apple slices with cinnamon.
2. Put them in the air fryer basket. Weigh them down with a metal rack to prevent from flying around the basket.
3. Cook on air fryer mode at 300°F for 16 minutes.
4. Allow to cool and crisp for at least 5 minutes before serving.

Serving suggestion

Consume immediately once crisp.

Tip

Store in an airtight container for later. The chips will soften when exposed in the air for too long.

Zucchini Pizza Boats

Preparation time
5 MINUTES

Cooking time
7 MINUTES

Servings
6

Ratings
★

Ingredients

3 medium zucchinis, halved

1/2 cup pizza sauce

4 cup mozzarella cheese, shredded

Directions

1. Scoop out the center of the zucchinis to make boats.
2. Fill in the center with pizza sauce and cheese.
3. Cook in the air fryer at 350°F for 7 minutes.
4. Plate and enjoy.

Serving suggestion

Top with more cheese and serve warm.

Tip

You can tweak this recipe to load your boat with other fillings of your choice.

Roasted Shishito Peppers

Preparation time
10 MINUTES

Cooking time
5 MINUTES

Servings
4

Ratings
★★★
★

Ingredients

2 tablespoons olive oil
Salt and pepper to taste
8 oz Shishito peppers

Directions

1. Rub the Shishito peppers with olive oil, salt and pepper.
2. Cook on roast setting at 380°F for 5 to 7 minutes.

Serving suggestion

Enjoy by itself, or with cornbread.

Tip

You may also dice them to garnish your salad or soup.

Garlic Carrot Fingers

Preparation time
10 MINUTES

Cooking time
12 MINUTES

Servings
4

Ratings
★★★
★

Ingredients

1 lb. carrot, peeled and cut
2 teaspoons garlic powder
Salt and pepper to taste
1 tablespoon olive oil

Directions

1. Coat the carrots by mixing all the ingredients.
2. Set the air fryer oven to roast mode at 390°F.
3. Roast for 10 to 12 minutes.

Serving suggestion

Garnish with parsley and cream cheese.

Tip

If you want a spicy version, just add ground cinnamon and chili powder into the mix.

Roasted Cauliflower

Preparation time
5 MINUTES

Cooking time
15 MINUTES

Servings
4

Ratings
★ ★ ★
★

Ingredients

1 tablespoon sesame oil
Salt and pepper to taste
1 head cauliflower florets
3 teaspoons garlic powder

Directions

1. Season the florets with sesame oil, salt, pepper, and garlic powder.
2. Roast in your air fryer oven at 400°F for 15 minutes.
3. Flip the florets halfway through.

Serving suggestion

Garnish with grated parmesan cheese.

Tip

You may also coat with panko breadcrumbs.

Black Bean Burger

Preparation time: 20 MINUTES | **Cooking time:** 15 MINUTES | **Servings:** 6

Ratings
★ ★ ★
★

Ingredients

- 16 oz. black beans, drained
- 1/2 cup corn kernels
- 1-1/3 cups rolled oats
- ¾ cup salsa
- 1/2 teaspoon garlic powder
- 1-1/4 teaspoons mild chili powder
- 1/2 teaspoon chipotle chili powder
- 1 tablespoon soy sauce

Directions

1. Except for the corn, blend all ingredients in a food processor.
2. Add the corn and refrigerate for 15 minutes.
3. Shape the mixture into patties.
4. Set the air fryer oven to bake mode at 375°F.
5. Bake for 15 minutes or until crispy.

Serving suggestion

Make a sandwich and serve with guilt-free air fryer fries.

Tip

Wrap the patties tightly and freeze for up to 3 months.

Crispy Falafel

Preparation time: 10 MINUTES

Cooking time: 15 MINUTES

Servings: 6

Ratings

★ ★ ★
★

Ingredients

2 cups dried chickpeas, soaked
1 tablespoon chickpea flour
3/4 cup parsley, chopped
1 medium onion, diced
1/4 cup cilantro, chopped
2 cloves garlic, minced
2 teaspoons ground coriander
2 teaspoons cumin powder
1/2 teaspoon cayenne pepper
Salt and pepper to taste

Directions

1. Blend together all the ingredients slightly in a food processor to make a coarse mixture.
2. Shape the mixture into 1.5-inch balls.
3. Arrange in a single layer on a lined baking pan.
4. Cook on bake mode at 370°F for 15 minutes or until crispy and golden brown.

Serving suggestion

Serve with tzatziki sauce.

Tip

You may soak the chickpeas overnight for best results.

Lamb and Goat Dishes

Roasted Lamb Chops with Garlic and Rosemary

Preparation time
30 MINUTES

Cooking time
15 MINUTES

Servings
4

Ratings

★★★
★

Ingredients

2 tablespoons olive oil
1 tablespoon fresh rosemary, chopped
4 cloves garlic, minced
Pepper to taste
8 lamb chops
Salt to taste

Directions

1. Combine olive oil, rosemary, garlic, and pepper in a bowl.
2. Coat lamb chops with mixture.
3. Marinate for 30 minutes at room temperature.
4. Line your baking sheet with foil.
5. Season lamb chops with salt.
6. Position the baking pan inside the air fryer oven.
7. Choose bake function.
8. Bake at 425°F for 15 minutes.

Serving suggestion

Garnish with rosemary sprigs.

Tip

You can also marinate lamb chops overnight.

Lamb chops with Fennel and Orange Salad

Preparation time: 15 MINUTES

Cooking time: 30 MINUTES

Servings: 4

Ratings: ★★★★

Ingredients

- 6 garlic cloves, minced
- 2 garlic heads, sliced crosswise
- 1 teaspoon orange zest, grated
- 1 teaspoon red pepper flakes
- 1 cup white wine
- 2 tablespoons rosemary, finely chopped
- 2 tablespoons lemon juice
- 2 tablespoons olive oil
- 1 cup orange, sliced
- 6 to 8 lamb chops
- 1 fennel bulb, thinly sliced
- Salt and pepper to taste

Directions

1. Score lamb with a sharp knife.
2. Season with salt and pepper.
3. Mix minced garlic, zest, olive oil, rosemary, and pepper flakes in a bowl.
4. Coat lamb with the mixture.
5. Place lamb in the baking pan together with garlic heads and wine. Cover with foil
6. Select the roast function.
7. Roast at 300°F for 30 minutes or until tender.
8. Mix fennel, orange slices, salt, and lemon juice in a bowl.
9. Serve with lamb chops.

Serving suggestion

Top lamb with rosemary.

Tip

Drizzle leftover juices over meat and salad.

Lamb Chops in Dijon Garlic

Preparation time	Cooking time	Servings
25 MINUTES	20 MINUTES	2

Ratings
★ ★ ★
★

Ingredients

8 pieces lamb chops
2 teaspoons Dijon mustard
1 teaspoon soy sauce
2 teaspoons olive oil
1 teaspoon cumin powder
1 teaspoon minced garlic
1 teaspoon cayenne powder
Salt to taste

Directions

1. Combine Dijon mustard, olive oil, cumin and cayenne powder, soy sauce, and garlic in a bowl.
2. Place lamb chops in a Ziploc bag together with the mixture.
3. Marinate for 30 minutes in the fridge.
4. Choose bake function.
5. Cook for 17 minutes at 350°F.

Serving suggestion

Add 3 minutes to the cooking time to make lamb chops well done.

Tip

You can also marinate the lamb chops overnight to save time.

Braised Lamb Shanks

Preparation time
10 MINUTES

Cooking time
2 HOUR 20 MINUTES

Servings
4

Ratings

★

Ingredients

4 garlic cloves, crushed
1-1/2 teaspoon kosher salt
3 cups beef broth
4 sprigs of fresh rosemary
4 lamb shanks
2 tablespoons balsamic vinegar
Salt and pepper to taste

Directions

1. Rub lamb with salt, pepper, garlic, and olive oil.
2. Place in baking pan with rosemary.
3. Select roast function.
4. Roast for 20 minutes at 425°F.
5. Turn lamb halfway while roasting.
6. Add the vinegar and 2 cups of broth and switch to slow cook.
7. Slow cook at 250°F for 1 hour.
8. Add remaining cup of broth and slow cook for another hour.

Serving suggestion

Garnish with fresh rosemary sprigs.

Tip

Lamb is ready when the meat easily pulls from the bone.

Roasted Lamb with Cumin and Lemon Crust

Preparation time: 15 MINUTES

Cooking time: 25 MINUTES

Servings: 3

Ratings: ★★★

Ingredients

1/2 cup breadcrumbs
1 egg, beaten
1 cloves garlic, grated
1 teaspoon cumin seeds
1/4 lemon rind, grated
1 teaspoon oil
1 teaspoon ground cumin
1.7 lb. rack of lamb, frenched
Salt
freshly ground black pepper to taste

Directions

1. Season lamb rack with salt and pepper.
2. Combine breadcrumbs, cumin seeds, garlic, ground cumin, oil, ½ teaspoon of salt, and lemon rind in a large bowl.
3. Dip the lamb in the egg then coat with the breadcrumb mixture until a crust is formed.
4. Arrange the lamb in the frying basket.
5. Choose the bake function.
6. Bake at 100°F for 25 minutes.
7. Switch to roast function.
8. Roast at 200°F for 5 minutes.
9. Remove from air fryer and cover with foil.
10. Leave alone for 10 minutes to rest before carving.

Serving suggestion

Serve with roasted vegetables or a fresh salad.

Tip

You can substitute Dijon mustard for the egg.

Lamb Rack with Potatoes and Yogurt Mint Sauce

Preparation time
10 MINUTES

Cooking time
20 MINUTES

Servings
2

Ratings
★★★★

Ingredients

2 teaspoons fresh rosemary, chopped
1 teaspoon paprika
1 bunch asparagus
1-1/2 tablespoon olive oil
1 red bell pepper, cut into strips
1/2 lb. potatoes, cut into wedges
1 lb. lamb rack
Salt and pepper to taste
1/2 bunch mint, finely chopped
2/3 cup Greek yogurt

Directions

1. Season lamb with salt, pepper, and rosemary.
2. Coat potatoes with 1 tablespoon oil, paprika, and pepper.
3. Arrange lamb and potatoes in the pan.
4. Select roast function.
5. Roast for 15 minutes at 400°F.
6. Remove lamb and potatoes from air fryer and cover with foil for 10 minutes before carving.
7. Mix bell pepper and asparagus with the remaining oil.
8. Roast for 6 minutes at 300°F.
9. Mix yogurt with mint.

Serving suggestion

Serve lamb and vegetables with yogurt sauce.

Tip

You can also add Dijon mustard as seasoning before roasting.

Lamb Kebabs

Preparation time
5 MINUTES

Cooking time
10 MINUTES

Servings
3

Ratings
★★★
★★

Ingredients

1 tablespoon extra-virgin olive oil

2 teaspoons cumin powder

1 lb. lamb fillet, cut into 1-inch pieces

Salt and fresh ground pepper to taste

Directions

1. Combine all the ingredients in a bowl.
2. Put 2 pieces of lamb onto 6-inch skewers.
3. Choose the air fry option.
4. Cook for 8 minutes at 400°F.
5. Flip halfway through the cooking time.

Serving suggestion

Serve with yogurt and mint sauce as finger food.

Tip

You can cook the lamb without the skewers and serve with pitta bread.

Spiced Lamb Chops with Garlic Yogurt sauce

Preparation time
30 MINUTES

Cooking time
10 MINUTES

Servings
4

Ratings
★★★★

Ingredients

1/4 teaspoon allspice powder
1 teaspoon coriander, ground
2 teaspoons cumin, ground
2 cloves garlic, grated
3/4 teaspoon turmeric, ground
1/2 lemon, squeezed
1-1/2 cups Greek yogurt
Salt and pepper to taste
Cooking oil
8 lamb chops

Directions

1. Whisk together yogurt, garlic, lemon, salt, and pepper in a bowl.
2. Transfer 1/2 of the yogurt mixture to a small bowl and set aside.
3. Add the cumin, allspice, coriander, and turmeric to the yogurt mixture and set aside.
4. Season lamb chops with salt and pepper.
5. Coat lamb with spiced yogurt.
6. Leave at room temperature for 30 minutes.
7. Choose the air fry option.
8. Lightly spray the pan with oil and put lamb.
9. Air fry at 400°F for 3 minutes on each side.
10. Serve with the garlic yogurt mixture.

Serving suggestion

Serve with a fresh salad or herbed mashed potatoes.

Tip

Spray a light coating of oil halfway through or after flipping the lamb.

Air Fryer Feta and Lamb Frittata

Preparation time: 5 MINUTES

Cooking time: 15 MINUTES

Servings: 4

Ratings: ★★★★

Ingredients

- 8 large eggs
- 1 garlic clove, grated
- 1 teaspoon lemon zest, grated
- 1/4 cup plain yogurt
- 4 oz. lamb, ground
- 1 teaspoon fresh lemon juice
- 2 scallions, thinly sliced
- 1/4 cup feta, crumbled
- 1 tablespoon tarragon leaves
- 2 cups baby kale
- 1 tablespoon za'atar
- 1/2 cup cilantro leaves
- 1/4 cup basil leaves, torn
- Mild red pepper flakes
- 3 tablespoons olive oil
- Salt
- freshly ground black pepper to taste

Directions

1. In a bowl, mix 1 tablespoon oil, za'atar, garlic, 1/2 teaspoon lemon zest, lemon juice, and lamb. Season with salt and pepper.
2. Combine yogurt, eggs, scallions, feta, basil, tarragon, cilantro, and kale.
3. Whisk mixture and season with salt and pepper.
4. Select the air fry option in your air fryer oven.
5. Lightly coat pan with oil and add lamb mixture.
6. Set temperature to 350°F and cook for at least 2 minutes or until golden brown.
7. Pour in the egg mixture.
8. With a rubber spatula, pull in the sides until it has set evenly.
9. Switch to bake function.
10. Bake at 300°F F for 10 minutes.

Serving suggestion

Top with yogurt and garnish with lemon zest, pepper, and herbs.

Tip

Frittata is ready when the center wobbles when shaken.

Grilled Rosemary Jerk Lamb Chops

Preparation time: 10 MINUTES

Cooking time: 4 HOURS 10 MINUTES

Servings: 6 - 8

Ratings: ★★★★

Ingredients

- 2 lb. lamb loin chops
- 1-1/2 tablespoons soy sauce
- 7 cloves garlic
- 1/3 cup scallions
- 1 sprig rosemary
- 1/2 Scotch bonnet chili
- 1/2 teaspoon allspice
- 1 medium yellow onion, chopped
- Salt and pepper to taste

Directions

1. To make the marinade, blend soy sauce, garlic, onion, scallions, rosemary, chili, and allspice until smooth.
2. Coat and massage lamb chops with marinade.
3. Cover and chill for 4 hours.
4. Choose the grill option.
5. Grill lamb at 400°F for 11 to 14 minutes.

Serving suggestion

Garnish with rosemary sprigs.

Tip

Lamb can be marinated overnight.

Grilled Lamb Chops with Tzatziki Sauce

Preparation time
1 HOUR

Cooking time
10 MINUTES

Servings
2

Ratings
★★★
★

Ingredients

4 lamb loin chops
3 tablespoons olive oil
1/2 teaspoon red chili flakes
1 tablespoon fresh lemon juice
2 teaspoons dried dill
8 cloves garlic, minced
3/4 cup plain Greek yogurt
1/2 cup cucumber, minced
Kosher salt and pepper to taste

Directions

1. To create tzatziki sauce, whisk yogurt, 2 cloves minced garlic, 1 teaspoon dill, 1 tablespoon lemon juice, cucumber, salt, and pepper. Cover and chill.
2. Combine the remaining dill, garlic, lemon juice, chili flakes, and oil in a bowl to create the marinade.
3. Spice up the lamb with salt and pepper and place in a baking tray.
4. Coat lamb with the marinade and leave at room temperature for 1 hour.
5. Choose the grill function in your air fryer.
6. Grill lamb at 350°F for 4 to 6 minutes (medium-rare).

Serving suggestion

Spread tzatziki sauce on a platter and lay lamb chops on top.

Tip

A simple fresh green salad goes well with this dish.

Spiced Lamb Chops with Ginger Soy Sauce

Preparation time
2 HOURS 15 MINUTES

Cooking time
15 MINUTES

Servings
8

Ratings
★★★

Ingredients

8 lamb rib chops
1/3 cup scallions, finely chopped
3 tablespoons shallot, minced
2 tablespoons cilantro, minced
2 tablespoons ginger, minced
2 tablespoons garlic, minced
3 tablespoons oyster sauce
1 tablespoon sugar
2 tablespoons light soy sauce
Steamed Bok choy
Salt and pepper to taste
Red and yellow bell peppers, julienned
Scallions, julienned

Directions

1. Combine oyster sauce, soy sauce, oil, cilantro, sugar, garlic, shallot, and ginger.
2. Add lamb chops and leave to marinate for 2 hours at room temperature.
3. Choose grill function in your air fryer.
4. Place lamb in tray and season with salt and pepper.
5. Grill chops at 400°F for 6 minutes.
6. Transfer to a platter and cover with foil.
7. Let sit for 10 minutes.
8. Pour marinade into the pan and cook for 8 minutes or until it is reduced to create the sauce.

Serving suggestion

Arrange steamed Bok choy in the plate and put lamb over together with julienned peppers and scallion. Serve with the sauce from the marinade.

Tip

To reduce preparation time, marinate the lamb overnight, and keep in the fridge.

Spicy Lamb with Lentils and Herbs

Preparation time: 20 MINUTES

Cooking time: 15 MINUTES

Servings: 4

Ratings: ★★★★

Ingredients

1/2 lb. ground lamb
2 garlic cloves, thinly sliced
1/2 teaspoon cumin seeds
3/4 cup plain Greek yogurt
1 teaspoon crushed red pepper flakes
1/2 cucumber, chopped
1/4 cup fresh parsley
1/2 cup fresh cilantro, chopped
1-1/2 cups French green lentils
1 tablespoon vegetable oil
Kosher salt and pepper to taste
Flatbread and lemon wedges

Directions

1. Season lamb with salt and pepper.
2. Place lamb on the baking sheet.
3. Choose the air fry option.
4. Air fry for 350°F for 5 minutes.
5. Break apart lamb and add red pepper flakes, cumin, and garlic.
6. Cook for 2 more minutes and set aside.
7. Season lentils with salt and pepper.
8. Put lentils in the baking pan and cook until brown for 6 minutes.
9. Add the lamb back and mix well.
10. Remove from heat and add parsley, cucumber, and cilantro.

Serving suggestion

Spread yogurt on the plate and put the lamb on top. Serve with the flatbread and lemon wedges.

Tip

Garnish with fresh parsley and cilantro leaves.

Salt and Pepper Lamb

Preparation time
25 MINUTES

Cooking time
15 MINUTES

Servings
4

Ratings
★★★

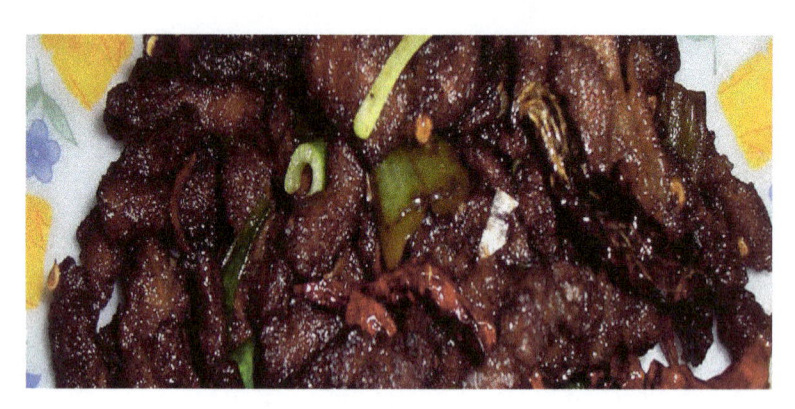

Ingredients

1-1/2 lb. lamb rump
4 oz. rice flour
3-1/2 oz. plain flour
3 egg whites
2 zucchinis, thinly sliced
1 red capsicum, sliced into strips
1 green capsicum, sliced into strips

Directions

1. Cut lamb into thin stripsacross the grain.
2. Combine flours in a bowl and season with salt and pepper.
3. Whisk eggs in a separate bowl.
4. Dip strips of lamb in the egg then onto the flour individually.
5. Lightly coat a baking tray with oil.
6. Select the air fry option.
7. Air fry lamb for 3 to 4 minutes at 350°F.
8. Set aside lamb.
9. In the same tray, arrange the capsicums and zucchinis.
10. Air fry for 2 to 3 minutes until tender and has light charring.

Serving suggestion

Serve lamb with charred vegetables, lime wedges, and mayonnaise

Tip

You can also add freshly chopped onions as garnish.

Barbecue Lamb Cutlets

Preparation time: 30 MINUTES

Cooking time: 40 MINUTES

Servings: 4

Ratings: ★★★★

Ingredients

2 cups tomato ketchup
1/2 cup white vinegar
2 teaspoons Tabasco sauce
3 teaspoons Worcestershire sauce
1/2 cup brown sugar
1 onion, finely chopped
2 teaspoons mild mustard
4 large potatoes, cut into wedges
3-1/2 oz. sour cream
3 tablespoons vegetable oil
2 tablespoons mint, chopped
Salt and pepper to taste
16 small lamb chops

Directions

1. To make the marinade, combine onion, ketchup, vinegar, Worcestershire sauce, tabasco sauce, and sugar.
2. Soak lamb cuts in the marinade for 1 hour in the refrigerator.
3. Mix oil with salt and pepper.
4. Coat potatoes with the oil mixture.
5. Choose the air fry option.
6. Air fry at 400°F for 25 minutes until crispy.
7. Set aside potatoes once cooked.
8. Take out lamb and place it in the baking tray.
9. For 15 minutes Air fry at 350°F.

Serving suggestion

Place 4 pieces of lamb on each plate. Serve with potato wedged topped with sour cream and garnished with mint leaves.

Tip

You can marinate the lamb overnight to save time.

Conclusion

Dear Reader,

I can tell you in all confidence that I have tested all the recipes above and have been satisfied not only with their excellent success but also with the performance of Emeril, without which I would not have achieved such results! That's why I have poured into this book all the experience and expertise accumulated during my culinary experiments, and that's why I am convinced I can help you solve many problems. At least in the kitchen!

;)

So go ahead and experiment with your Emeril Lagasse air fryer, and remember: your imagination is the first and most valuable ingredient in any recipe!

Ciro

Lightning Source UK Ltd.
Milton Keynes UK
UKHW050949150621
385540UK00002B/7

9 781803 217925